Tyntesfield

Wraxall,
North Somerset

Supported by

The National Lottery®
through the Heritage Lottery Fund

heritage
lottery fund

National Trust

Tyntesfield unveiled

Only ten weeks after taking formal possession of Tyntesfield, the National Trust's voluntary guides began showing groups around the ground floor of the house. Rather than shrouding the house in scaffolding for three or four years followed by a self-congratulatory unveiling in five years' time, the Trust is determined to involve the public, as well as experts, in the excitement of discovery and in the challenges of conservation. Wherever possible, it is hoped to involve the wider public in the processes necessary to bring the house back to life, for Tyntesfield can not only entertain and inspire, it can offer life-enhancing opportunities to learn.

The past preserved

At Tyntesfield, four generations of the Gibbs family each made changes, but always with unusual sympathy for their predecessors' work. Furthermore, in the second half of the last century, fewer

servants were matched by far fewer guests and, consequently, by diminishing wear and tear. Original carpets, fabrics, wallpapers and stencilling have also survived here for more than a century, partly because blinds and shutters were closed against the sunlight. When a fireplace or carpet was replaced, the old one was often carefully stored away. And the late Lord Wraxall conscientiously kept the house and gardens in good order, repairing roofs and maintaining the kitchen garden in full production.

The exceptionally well-preserved servants' quarters at Tyntesfield, together with the stables, the extensive kitchen gardens, lodges, sawmill, and the home farm and many other estate buildings, are matched by a vast and largely unexplored archive through which the daily life

(Below) All the implements of a vanished world of service survive at Tyntesfield

(Above) The garden front as illustrated in The Builder *in 1866, the year after John Norton's rebuilding for William Gibbs. The clock tower was demolished in 1935*

Conservation in the community

Right from the start, the National Trust was determined to give people access to Tyntesfield and the conservation process rather than wait until everything was finished. This saw a 'cobwebs and all' approach when pre-booked guided tours began in October 2002, before Tyntesfield opened with temporary facilities in late 2005. We like people to be as involved as possible, creating opportunities to learn new skills, while ensuring conservation techniques are passed to the next generation. In the first six years many thousands of people have been involved as volunteers, students or as part of community groups. We look forward to increasing opportunities as facilities improve.

Ruth Gofton, *Property Manager*

and work of the household, the servants and the estate workers can be rediscovered. This interim guide has had to depend largely on secondary knowledge and will need to be rewritten after the archive has been studied. The scope of the guide will also be extended as more of the house and the estate are opened or made accessible to visitors.

Competing pressures

The pressure from the public eager to visit Tyntesfield is both heartening and threatening. The character of a property can be as fragile as its contents, and the preservation of one can often be at odds with the conservation of the other. The National Trust is finding ways of increasing the number of visitors, whilst at the same time preserving both the contents and the friendly and enthralling character of this house. It is a challenge that the Trust is committed to undertaking openly and jointly with volunteers, students, trainees, visitors and many other groups.

'Tenacious of purpose': the Gibbs family

The spectacular rebuilding of Tyntesfield, completed in 1865, was undertaken by William Gibbs when he was well into his seventies and many years after his fortune was secure. It was a proud and affectionate tribute to his family, to the labours of his forebears, and to his deep religious faith.

William's grandfather was George Abraham Gibbs (1718–94), an Exeter surgeon and owner of Pytte, an estate at Clyst St George, near Exeter, which had belonged to his ancestors since 1560. George Abraham's youngest son, Antony (William's father), was apprenticed to a local merchant trading with Spain, before developing his own business, exporting woollen cloth. In 1789 that business failed disastrously, prompting the bankruptcy of his father, his principal investor. The cause is still not clear, but Antony blamed no one but himself and his own personal failings. He now submitted himself to a life of unremitting industry. 'God in his mercy,' he wrote later to his father, 'grant that you may live to see me expiate in some measure by the steadiness of my present conduct for the folly of what is past.'

Soon after the failure, Antony moved to Spain, acting as an agent for British manufacturers and merchants, and in due course setting up as a merchant in his own right. His adored wife, Dorothea Barnetta Hucks, their daughter, Harriett, and elder son, George Henry, known as Henry, soon followed him to Madrid. There, William was born on 22 May 1790.

Antony Gibbs & Sons

In 1805 war drove Antony from Spain, leaving a substantial amount of seemingly unsaleable stock blockaded in Cadiz. With the vital assistance of his brother, Vicary, then Solicitor-General in Pitt's last government, he succeeded in getting a licence to carry his goods in a Spanish ship to Lima in Peru, where Spain had a monopoly of trade. This venture eventually produced a modest profit, assisting Antony in the formal establishment of Antony Gibbs & Sons in London in 1808 and laying down vital links with South America.

When Antony died in 1815, his elder son Henry was effectively managing the business in London, and William was successfully and most conscientiously running the business in Cadiz. Both the foundations and the reputation of the firm were now well established.

Antony's life and conduct had fulfilled the family's motto, *Tenax propositi* ('tenacious of purpose'). And it undoubtedly inspired his sons Henry and William, who in 1818 set up a special 'D. S. account', standing for *deudas sagradas* ('sacred debts') in order to pay off the creditors in their father's original business. There was no legal obligation on them; these were debts of honour only, which were finally paid off in 1840, just over 50 years after the bankruptcy. The Gibbs family's roots were also restored in 1859, when William bought back Pytte, the family home, which his grandfather had been forced to sell in 1790.

William Gibbs (1790–1875)

William had been sent to Blundell's Grammar School at Tiverton in 1800. As early as 1802, at the age of twelve, he first joined his father for nine months to assist him with his business in Cadiz. Early in 1806, still aged only fifteen, William became a clerk in the Bristol counting house of Gibbs, Bright & Gibbs, headed by his uncle, George Gibbs. Two years later he joined his family, now in London, working as a clerk to the Portuguese Commissioners. Within a few months he had seven or eight clerks under him. He was also soon working increasingly in his father's office, finally becoming a partner in 1813.

From 1813 to 1822 William was an almost constant resident of Cadiz. His return to England marked a decline in the Spanish business and a steady increase in the South America trade. However, not until the 1830s were steady profits, at last, to be made. It was in these years that William's brother, Henry, the senior partner, was so closely involved with the promotion and development of the Great Western Railway, championing Brunel in boardroom battles.

(Above) William Gibbs of Tyntesfield; painted by William Boxall in 1859 (Hall Gallery)

(Right) Guano mining on the Chincha islands off Peru about 1870. The profits from this industry paid for the building of Tyntesfield

(Left) Antony and Dorothea Gibbs, by George Drown after John Downman, 1784

In 1842 Henry died during a visit to Venice. William was now head, and for several years sole partner, of Antony Gibbs & Sons. 1842 was also the year in which the firm's South American agent took out government contracts for the shipment of guano (solidified bird droppings) from the barren islands off Peru. William, alarmed by the accompanying loans, called it an 'act of insanity'. However, it was the firm's virtual monopoly in the trade of this potent agricultural fertiliser and the efforts of the Chinese indentured labourers who mined it that were to turn William from a successful merchant into a man of immense wealth.

William remained head of Antony Gibbs & Sons until his death in 1875 in his 85th year. Within the firm he had come to be known, affectionately, as 'Prior', perhaps a reference not only to his increasing preoccupation with religious matters, but, at last, to a certain detachment from day-to-day management. It was his nephew, Henry Hucks Gibbs (created 1st Lord Aldenham in 1896), who now steered the company. And it was probably Henry, when he was Governor of the Bank of England, at whom the City's well-known jingle was directed: 'Mr Gibbs made his dibs, selling the turds of foreign birds.'

William and Blanche

In 1839 William married Matilda Blanche Crawley-Boevey (1817–87), daughter of Sir Thomas Crawley-Boevey of Flaxley Abbey in Gloucestershire. At the age of 49 he was marrying a woman of 21.

William and Blanche (as Matilda Blanche was usually known) lived first in London, where their seven children were born. From 1851 their London house was 16 Hyde Park Gardens, for which some of the pictures and furniture now at Tyntesfield were acquired. As the family grew, the appeal of a country residence must have increased. William's sister was living at Belmont, a few miles south-west of Bristol, and there were other relations in Bristol and

Gloucestershire. The opening of the Great Western Railway to Bristol in 1841 may also have influenced their decision. In 1843 William's diaries record several visits to Tyntesfield while staying at Belmont, less than a mile away along the hill and originally part of the same estate. In the same year the widow of the Rev. George Turner Seymour, the builder of Tyntesfield c.1813–20, sold the property to William, and the purchase may have been completed by April of the following year.

(Right) William and Blanche Gibbs with five of their children, painted by Sir William Ross in 1849

William and Blanche Gibbs with their family in 1862–3. The house chaplain, the Rev. John Hardie, is seated at the table

The large and beautiful portrait miniatures on ivory by Sir William Ross, who stayed at the house for six weeks in 1849, suggest Tyntesfield's cheerful family life. A carefully posed and inevitably rather stilted studio photograph of the family, probably taken in 1862–3 during the rebuilding, includes the family chaplain and perhaps the family doctor as well as six of the seven children. William, with his youngest daughter, Albinia, on his knees, looks almost impish, but Blanche's dour glance seems almost to anticipate her husband's anxious diary entry for 6 October 1865, written after that first long summer of showing friends and relations around the new house: 'Painful talk to Blanchey who seems so dreadfully depressed and tired for having people in the house that I shall be afraid to ask anyone to come here.'

The novelist Charlotte M. Yonge, a cousin of both William and Blanche, often stayed at Tyntesfield after the rebuilding. She recalled, 'That beautiful home was like a church in spirit, I used to think so when going up and down the great staircase like a Y. At the bottom, after prayers, Mr Gibbs in his wheeled chair used to wish everybody goodnight, always keeping the last kiss for his "little maid", Albinia, with her brown eyes and rich shining hair.'

A pastel portrait of Blanche drawn in the last year of her life justly depicts a lady of great warmth and dignity. Closely involved with her husband's innumerable church projects during his life, her twelve years at Tyntesfield as a widow saw further contributions to the local community. A large village club was built, as well as a cottage convalescent home, an almshouse and Wraxall's Battle Axes Inn, which Blanche established in her own name on the principles of temperance rather than teetotalism. St Michael's Home for Consumptives above Axbridge (now a Cheshire Home), which William Butterfield designed, was built in her husband's memory.

Antony Gibbs (1841–1907)

William and Blanche's eldest son was brought up at Tyntesfield and educated privately and at Radley before going up to Exeter College, Oxford, in 1860. It was the year in which Exeter's new chapel by George Gilbert Scott was consecrated and just seven years after both Burne-Jones and William Morris had entered the college. Watercolours of Antony's Oxford rooms show the walls crowded with pictures, suggesting that he was already a serious collector.

William Gibbs is said to have recommended against Antony's entry into the family business after establishing that he was unable to add up four columns of figures simultaneously. Instead, Antony became a local magistrate, continued his parents' charitable and religious concerns, managed his estates and pursued his sporting, antiquarian and collecting interests. He was an outstanding turner of wood and ivory,

Antony Gibbs with his wife Janet Louisa (on the right) and her sister Sophy Merivale

These intricately turned ivory candlesticks were the work of Antony Gibbs

a fashionable pastime for Victorian gentlemen. The complicated spiral twists on the candlesticks mounted with ancient intaglios and carved coral demonstrate the exceptional sophistication of his work.

In 1869 Antony moved into Charlton, a large Tudor house a mile or so away over the brow of the hill, which his father had acquired in 1865. It is now the Downs School. Perhaps as a consequence of his many journeys up and down the hill between Tyntesfield and Charlton, Antony invented a bicycle that stored energy when going downhill, which it then released when going uphill. Unfortunately, it was rather heavy-going on the flat and has not survived. He also learnt to play the organ, later introducing one to the oratory in Tyntesfield, now known as the Organ Room.

Antony married Janet Louisa Merivale in 1872 in SS Michael and All Angels, Exeter, a church which Antony's father had recently

Antony Gibbs's three eldest children, Albinia, Antony and George, painted by Edward Clifford in January 1878

built. Janet was to have ten children between 1873 and 1889. The delightful watercolour portrait by Edward Clifford, completed in 1878, of the three eldest children was painted when the family was still at Charlton. It has a suggestion of the view north from the house with the Severn estuary in the distance and the Welsh hills beyond.

Antony's mother, Matilda Blanche Gibbs, died in 1887 at the age of 69, and after very substantial alterations, Antony and his family moved down to Tyntesfield in the summer of 1890. Antony had first spent a trial night in the house testing 'all the new-fangled electric lights'. His architect was Henry Woodyer, whom he had earlier employed at Charlton and who had also designed the veranda at Tyntesfield for his mother. Woodyer's alterations included the enlargement of the Dining Room and Billiard Room and radical changes to the halls and the staircase. Antony's changes cost over £50,000, not so far from his father's total costs of just over £70,000 for the virtual rebuilding of the house.

The bronze throne was made in 1877 by Barkentin & Krall for Antony Gibbs to a design by the great French Gothic Revival architect Viollet-le-Duc

George Abraham Gibbs in his uniform as Treasurer of the Royal Household

George Abraham Gibbs, 1st Lord Wraxall (1873–1931)

Soldier, politician and courtier, he inherited Tyntesfield on the death of his father in 1907. He had been elected to Parliament for the first time a year earlier and was to be MP for West Bristol until his elevation to the peerage in 1928.

Born at Charlton in 1873, he was sent to Eton and in 1892 went up to Christ Church, Oxford,

becoming Master of the Christ Church Beagles. He was a keen sportsman – cricket, racquets, hunting and shooting, especially.

George's time at university was interrupted by his commission in the North Somerset Yeomanry in 1893. After completing his degree, he later served in the South African War and was present at the capture of Pretoria in 1900, when he commanded Lord Roberts's body-guard. From 1914 to 1917 Colonel Gibbs raised and commanded the 2nd Regiment of the North Somerset Yeomanry.

In 1907 George married Via – Victoria Florence de Burgh Long. He was to be Parliamentary Private Secretary to his father-in-law, Walter Long, who was Secretary of State for the Colonies. He later became a government chief whip and was appointed a Privy Councillor in 1923. In 1921 he was made Treasurer of the Royal Household, an office he held with a brief break until 1928, when he was created Baron Wraxall of Clyst St George in Devon.

George seems to have moved in higher social circles than his father: among the guests he invited for country-house weekends at Tyntesfield were members of the government. Perhaps with this in mind, George and Via carried out important changes to the interior, most notably to the Drawing Room and to Mrs Gibbs's Room, but also to many of the bedrooms. Antony's important collection of maiolica was sold, and much comfortable and sumptuously upholstered 'antique furniture' was acquired, often in the Queen Anne style.

(Right) George and Via Gibbs installed the Renaissance Revival fireplace in Mrs Gibbs's Room

Via, who was appointed CBE for her services to the Red Cross, died in 1920 at the age of 39. An effusive and frustratingly uninformative biography justly states that she 'literally squandered her life in the service of others and never counted the cost'. More expressive are the awkward but touching words on her memorial in Tyntesfield Chapel, surely composed by her husband: 'Her wonderful personality and splendid sympathy made her greatly loved by all at Tyntesfield.' She seems to have enjoyed the gift of appearing to be at ease with anyone and everyone. Her two sons died in infancy, but her daughter, Doreen, who died in 2008, was a source of vital information about life at Tyntesfield.

In 1927 George Gibbs remarried, his bride being the Hon. Ursula Mary Lawley (1888–1979), daughter of the 6th Baron Wenlock. Ursula had been Maid of Honour to the Queen from 1912 to 1927, and King George V and Queen Mary attended their wedding at St Margaret's, Westminster. Ursula's two sons were born in 1928 and 1929, but in 1931, after only four years of marriage, her husband died.

George Richard Lawley Gibbs, 2nd Lord Wraxall (1928–2001)

He succeeded to the title at the age of only three, and it was his mother, Ursula, Lady Wraxall, who presided at Tyntesfield until her death in 1979. She had nursed in France during the First World War and was appointed OBE in 1945 for her services to the Red Cross during the Second World War. Her second son, the present Lord Wraxall, well remembers the hands-on efficiency with which she managed the farm and a multitude of chickens during the last war. At this time boarders from Clifton High School were lodged in the house, and American soldiers were convalescing in temporary housing in the grounds. The books in the Library were replaced with bandages and other medical equipment, for which the house was a regional distribution centre managed by Lady Wraxall.

The 2nd Lord Wraxall (known as Richard) went to Eton and served with the Coldstream Guards, before taking up the care of the estates and developing a keen expertise in forestry. He zealously maintained the gardens, kitchen

Lady Wraxall with her sons, Richard and Eustace; by John Arthur Machray

*(Left)
The Flaxley Bedroom in 2001*

*(Right)
Victorian plant labels and picture frames – the accumulation of 150 years at Tyntesfield*

gardens and the immediately surrounding land, when retrenchment might have been expected. He added to the picture collection but also sold some major items, including his grandfather's Turner and important pieces of Victorian furniture. However, the comprehensive and violent reaction against High Victorian art that stripped the interiors of so many Victorian country houses barely affected Tyntesfield.

He never married and, when he died unexpectedly at Tyntesfield in July 2001, he was alone. No one else was living in the house, and the main reception rooms were mostly shuttered and closed up. The title passed to his younger brother, Eustace, who has had a distinguished career as a diplomat.

The National Trust acquires Tyntesfield

In accordance with Lord Wraxall's will, the estate and the house were put on the market in April 2002, and it was announced that the contents would be sold by public auction in September. The National Trust had 50 days to raise over £20 million and to reach a very complex agreement with the executors acting on behalf of the nineteen heirs and beneficiaries.

Only very, very occasionally in recent years had the house been opened to visiting groups or special charity events. However, the National Trust was well aware that this was the last major High Victorian house and estate in private hands to have survived in a largely unaltered state and still with much of its original furnishings. The response to the news of Lord Wraxall's death was immediate, and as soon as access was permitted, expert feasibility reports were made and carefully considered.

The purchase was made possible by the public's remarkable response to the intense fund-raising campaign and to very favourable publicity. There have been over 77,000 individual contributions, and they are still coming in. A local bus driver raised £1,500 from passengers on his route which passed close to Tyntesfield – all the more remarkable as you cannot see the house from the road. American servicemen, who had been hospitalised at Tyntesfield during the last war, also contributed. Two benefactors gave separate donations of £1 million and £4 million.

Inspired by the breadth of public support, the National Heritage Memorial Fund made the crucial donation of £17.425 million, the largest single grant in its history and equivalent to three years' expenditure. The NHMF had been set up following the failure to save another exceptional Victorian house and its contents, Mentmore in Buckinghamshire, in 1980. It absorbed the National Land Fund, which had been created after the Second World War as a memorial to those who gave their lives for their country.

The executors' decision to accept the National Trust's offer for the house, much of the immediately surrounding estate and most of the contents was taken on 7 June 2002. The exchange of contracts took place on Saturday 15 June after a final marathon meeting lasting over 26 hours. It was an extraordinary feat, involving, for example, the Inland Revenue, which completed its review of heritage property-tax relief in four days, a procedure that normally takes at least three to four months. The National Trust took formal possession of Tyntesfield on 31 July 2002.

Tour of the House

The Exterior

The building that William Gibbs acquired in 1843 was a largely symmetrical country house built in around 1813–20, its flat surfaces articulated with simple Gothic detailing. Glimpses of this house can be seen, particularly within the south front's central block and the inner courtyard. Although much redecoration took place in the 1850s, it was not until William and Blanche had been living at Tyntesfield for twenty years that the extensive rebuilding took place.

The Regency house which William Gibbs bought in 1843 and transformed in Gothic Revival style in the 1860s

The architect was John Norton, and the date on all the drainpipe hoppers is 1864. Norton was a Bristol-born architect with offices in both Bristol and London. He was a pupil of Benjamin Ferrey, the friend and biographer of Augustus Welby Northmore Pugin, the most important and influential architect of the Gothic Revival.

Norton built up a large practice in church and country-house building. Of his six churches in Bristol, Holy Trinity, Stapleton, and St Mary Magdalene, Stoke Bishop, survive, as do the tower of Emmanuel church in Guthrie Road, Clifton, and the fine tower and steeple of Christ Church, Clifton. Norton had built some rather smaller country houses before Tyntesfield, but some very grand mansions such as Elveden Hall in Suffolk, built for a maharaja, and a castle in Estonia were to follow.

(Left) The east (entrance) front

Norton's Gothic is confident, individual and knowledgeable. At Tyntesfield the composition is asymmetrical with a lively picturesque outline. It was originally livelier still, with a more distinctly continental character. There was a tall square tower with a gas-lit clock over the entrance. It had a very steep pitched roof with sharp pinnacled turrets at each corner and coloured tiles in a strong diaper pattern, reminiscent of the medieval architecture of Burgundy. It was demolished in 1935.

Norton took excellent advantage of the outstanding London builders, William Cubitt & Sons, and the quality of the pointing of the Bath stone is exceptional. An impressive variety of materials was employed. The turret on the main garden front next to the Library roof has a candle-snuffer spire covered in ribbed lead, but the truncated bedroom turret nearest to the Chapel once had – and must surely have again – a spire covered in tiles in a diaper pattern. The Library, Drawing Room and entrance roofs, on the other hand, are covered with heavy stone slabs from the quarries at Box in Wiltshire.

The Porch

Carved above the entrance porch are the coats of arms of William Gibbs's parents, together with the Spanish motto: EN DIOS MI AMPARO Y ESPERANZA ('I place my trust in God'). We are reminded that William was born in Madrid and worked in Spain for many years, as well as of his deep affection for his parents and his profound faith. There are also the words: PAX INTRANTIBUS SALUS EXEUNTIBUS ('Peace to those who enter, fare well to those who depart'). It is a friendly welcome, much enhanced by the character of the stone carving.

As well as the exotic medieval beasts amongst the gargoyles, there is much excellent naturalistic carving, by a certain Mr Beates. Sheltering in the ferns on one of the capitals to the porch, for example, are lizards, dragonflies and even a dormouse, and the corbels to the porch's vault include cobnuts, holly and mistletoe, primroses and other flowers.

The Interior

Many of the contents were moved around after Lord Wraxall's death. As our knowledge of them increases, the contents and arrangement of rooms will continue to change.

The Cloister

In 1865 the Porch and the space under the tower were open to the elements. The front door was today's inner doors. Beyond, as now, was the entrance hall or 'cloister', the floor covered with fine encaustic tiles. Here were the existing cast-iron umbrella stands and coat hooks.

The impressive *hallstand*, dated 1878, bears the initials of William's widow, Matilda Blanche Gibbs, who had commissioned it from the Warwick cabinetmakers Collier and Plucknett.

(Above)
The hallstand was made for Blanche Gibbs in 1878 by the Warwick cabinetmakers Collier and Plucknett

The Library

The Library

The hinge bars to the door are inscribed: LITERA SCRIPTA MANET / VERBA LOCUTA VOLANT ('The written word remains; the spoken word floats away'). The mellow colours of the gold-tooled book bindings, the richer colours of the original carpet, the cheerful Minton tiles in the window seats, Norton's Gothic fireplaces and open oak roof – all contribute to the room's particular character.

In January 1866 – a month after the family moved back into the house following the rebuilding – the room was fitted out for family theatricals, which, no doubt, took advantage of the bay window at the far end of the room. This was never a sombre library, but a favourite family sitting room, loved and enjoyed by successive generations with the minimum of changes. Every flat surface was peopled with family photographs, which the National Trust hopes to replicate.

Furniture and contents

The deep-buttoned and upholstered sofa and *the two round-backed armchairs* of about 1855 retain their original wool and silk fabric. These are, like the carpet, by J. G. Crace & Son, one of the most important firms of decorators in 19th-century Britain. Much of the furniture and the curtains are early 20th-century. The current arrangement is inspired by a 1912 photograph.

Books

This is a very rare surviving example of a High Victorian gentleman's library – collected with a purpose and meant for use. The book stacks are carefully numbered in Latin numerals starting to the right of the window opposite the door with i, FINE ART, and ending, to the left of the window, with xvii, THEOLOGY. (Stacks xiii–xvi seem to have been removed later.)

William Gibbs was a man of great religious sensibility, and here are not only large numbers of Bibles and Prayer Books, but also the main texts of the Oxford Movement, which from the 1830s was intent upon reforming and revitalising the Church of England (see p. 30). It coincided with the Gothic Revival, and the seminal works of that architectural style are shelved under FINE ART. Here are the works of A.W. N. Pugin. Pugin emphasised the close association of the Gothic style with Christianity and argued that it was the true indigenous architecture of northern Europe. John Ruskin, too, came to argue that Gothic was the only 'proper' style for contemporary English architecture. All his major books are here.

There are substantial collections of 19th-century biography, classics, history, poetry, fiction and science. The Rev. J. B. Medley acted as librarian, compiling a printed catalogue in 1894.

Painting

Rent Day is by J. A. B. Stroebel, 1872.

Porcelain

The rare deep blue five-piece garniture on the chimneypiece was made in 1790 for the Chinese Imperial Palace. The spectacular display on the end wall is of Japanese Imari ware c.1700–20. The Chinese blue-and-white chargers are Kangxi period, c.1700.

The Dining Room

Above the door opposite the entrance to the Dining Room is the date 1889. After Blanche's death in 1887, her son, Antony, immediately began extensive, sensitive and very costly changes to Tyntesfield's interior. His architect was Henry Woodyer.

The individuality of Woodyer's work is demonstrated by the exuberance of the stone carving around the entrance to the Dining Room and by the superb bronze door furniture. He lengthened the Dining Room by extending it into the former housekeeper's room at the far end and widened it by replacing a single large bay window with the sequence of three bays. Above the columns he added Antony's initials and the family motto *Tenax propositi*. A frieze of heraldic lions runs all around the room, and the wooden ceiling is cleverly integrated into the room by the panelled surround to Norton's original marble fireplace, which Woodyer moved a little further down the room. The word 'welcome' is carved into the surround just below the mirror.

The wallpaper, lacquered, gilded and pressed to give it relief, is in imitation of tooled leather in the Spanish 'Cordolova' style. Although still sumptuous in effect, the lacquer has darkened, and the gilding has consequently lost its richness. Furthermore, at some time, the crimson background has been most laboriously filled in by hand with an off-white paint in the vain hope of lightening the overall effect. The carpet is English, of Turkish Smyrna design, *c.*1890.

The Dining Room

Furniture

The lower part of the *great carved oak sideboard* is by Crace and datable to 1855/6. The top part was commissioned by William and Blanche's son, Antony, around 1890 and is probably by James Plucknett.

The two carved oak side-tables flanking the fireplace and the four X-frame chairs are also by J. G. Crace. More obviously in the manner of A. W. N. Pugin, they remind us that Crace had worked closely with Pugin on furnishing the new Houses of Parliament and on the hugely successful Medieval Court at the Great Exhibition of 1851.

The elegant walnut chairs, made about 1900 by Charles Baker of Bath in the style of the 1720s, were probably acquired by George and Via Gibbs.

Paintings

The Floating Harbour, Bristol, is by J. B. Pyne. *Sunset on the Thames near Westminster with the New Houses of Parliament* is by Henry Dawson, 1875.

(Right, top) The carved stone doorway to the Dining Room was designed by Henry Woodyer for Antony Gibbs in the late 1880s

(Right) The lower part of the carved sideboard in the Dining Room was designed by Crace in 1855/6 and is decorated with William and Blanche Gibbs's initials

Henry Woodyer (1816–96), the first Old Etonian to practise as a professional architect, had worked with William Butterfield, and amongst his earlier buildings were the church and almshouses of St Raphael in Cumberland Road, Bristol. Built as a seamen's mission, it became so High Church that the chaplain's licence was revoked. Woodyer had also worked for Sir William Taylor Coleridge, one of William Gibbs's closest friends, and the great majority of his clients were to be devout High Churchmen. Henry Martin Gibbs, Antony's younger brother, was also employing Woodyer in the late 1880s on the sensitive restoration of Barrow Gurney church just across the valley and on Barrow Court, his Tudor country house.

The Lobby and Hall

Norton's long vestibule was extended to the hall by removing his carved and glazed screen and marble and tile mosaic floor, and installing the parquet-bordered floor. Carved doorways to the Oak and Dining rooms were created.

In 1889 Antony Gibbs made a series of practical changes to Norton's original design, which Woodyer imaginatively carried through with due respect for what had gone before. The main hall is a vast and impressive space. It is thirteen metres up to the ridge beam of Norton's open roof of English oak above the clerestory windows. Norton also designed the *fireplace* of Mansfield stone with its statues of Fortitude, Truth, Temperance, Justice and Prudence.

Norton's *staircase*, which rose from the centre of the hall, was moved against the farther wall, and the gallery was extended around the sides, improving access to the bedrooms. Woodyer reused Norton's fine staircase ironwork and his columns of green Connemara marble and Cornish serpentine, although the gasoliers that rose from the foot and angles of the staircase were succeeded by hanging electric lights, which have themselves since been replaced.

On the ground floor eight doors originally opened on to adjoining rooms or corridors. These were halved in number, making better use of the vestibule and Ante-Room.

Furniture

The *bronze armchair* with rock-crystal lion heads was made in 1877 by Barkentin & Krall for Antony Gibbs from a design by the leading French Gothic Revival architect Viollet-le-Duc. It is a considerable rarity in England.

Sculpture

The two full-length statues depict William and Blanche's two younger daughters, Alice and Albinia, both of whom were to die before their parents. The statues were commissioned in Rome during the Gibbs's continental tour in 1861–2, and William's diary confirms that Alice had at least eight sittings with Benjamin Edward Spence for the larger of the two statues.

It is a version of Spence's 1854 statue of *Highland Mary* (now at Osborne) depicting Mary Morrison, the unattainable love of Robert Burns. Lawrence Macdonald's more ideal statue of the eight-year-old Albinia holding a dove was commissioned only a few days before their departure from Rome. Fittingly, it now stands near a portrait of Albinia's father, who loved her so dearly and who must have been especially saddened by her death from TB in the last months of his life.

While in Rome William also commissioned Macdonald to do the fine *portrait busts* of himself and Matilda Blanche. A year earlier he had purchased *the busts of classical nymphs* by Richard James Wyatt, a pupil of Canova.

Portraits

Blanche by W. C. Horsley (1888) was commissioned soon after her death, from a drawing by Edward Clifford. William is depicted both half- and full-length with his walking stick (1859, gallery) by Sir William Boxall. George Abraham Gibbs first hung the portraits around the staircase gallery and in 1908 commissioned from A. H. Collings the grandest of the family portraits, of both himself and of his first wife, Via. George proudly wears the uniform of a Colonel of the North Somerset Yeomanry, with which he had served in South Africa. His father, Antony (with gun, 1879), is by J. H. Lorimer. *George as a child with brother Antony and sister Albinia* is by Edward Clifford.

Landscapes and Old Masters

William and Matilda Gibbs first acquired a major group of paintings following their visit to Spain in 1853. The great *St Laurence* attributed to Zambrano, which overlooks the Hall, was then believed to be by the more famous Spanish painter Zurbarán.

There is a significant number of coastal scenes – understandably, perhaps, for a family whose fortune was made from maritime trade. Most impressive are the enormous *Passage Boats* and *Luggage* by Sir Augustus Wall Callcott, bought by William in 1861, and *A Breezy Day on the English Coast* (showing St Michael's Mount) by Thomas Creswick and Richard Ansdell.

The Hall

The Ante-Room

According to the *Builder*, this was originally designed as an 'ante-room for sculpture'. The six statues now in the Hall were all acquired by William Gibbs in the early 1860s. **The tapestries** were woven by the Royal Windsor Tapestry Company in 1887 for Antony Gibbs. They depict scenes from the life of King Alfred and were intended as tributes to the memory of Antony's parents.

The Drawing Room

The ornately carved doors are both hinged and sliding – at a formal reception they could disappear into the wall altogether.

George and Via Gibbs moved into Tyntesfield soon after Antony's death in 1907. Their most radical alterations were to this room, which they used for formal entertaining. It was redecorated in Italian Renaissance style. In 1908 the carved fireplace was commissioned from Guido Minerbi in Venice, complete with the Gibbs coat of arms, and replaced Norton's vast mirror and Gothic fireplace. Crace's colourful stencilling on the walls and ceiling was replaced by the red damask with wide cut-silk velvet borders.

In 2004 staff and volunteers hung the pictures (collected by four generations of Gibbs) and rearranged the room in the Edwardian manner.

Furniture

Seventeenth- and 18th-century furniture, genuine and reproduction, reflects fashionable Edwardian taste. The finest is a rare 18th-century ivory-inlaid Indian table.

Pictures

The triple portrait of Charles I's children is a copy dated 1696 after Van Dyck. The 17th-century *Immaculate Conception* (right of fireplace, centre) is by Alonso De Tovar. The *Madonna and Child with St Zacharias, the Magdalen and St John* (left of fireplace, centre) is 16th-century, after Parmigianino.

The Drawing Room before rearrangement

Bedford Lemere's photograph of the Drawing Room in 1878 is a precious record of its original appearance. In the foreground is the Flaxley casket, a northern European ivory casket covered with carved ivory panels illustrating the Romance of the Knight of the Swan. It was considered to be 14th-century and it was one of the treasures of Flaxley Abbey, the family home of Matilda Blanche Gibbs. The casket was first identified as of later 18th-century date in 1968 by the Curator of Sculpture at the Rijksmuseum, Amsterdam. It is essentially an early fake and of much the same date as Thomas Chatterton's famous forgeries, written in Bristol in the 1770s, and of other early imitations of medieval art and literature. As such, it is a fascinating example of the rise of antiquarianism and of the Gothic Revival itself.

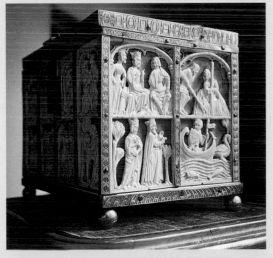

The Flaxley Abbey casket

The Organ Room

When William Gibbs planned the rebuilding of Tyntesfield, there were no proposals for a chapel. Instead there was this room, the oratory, where daily prayers were held. It was panelled in oak with oak stalls seating 50 people, and it had an organ, lectern and litany desk, and grisaille glass in the windows. Outside, two carved stone angels between the arches of the windows still announce the original function of the room. The entrance was from the Hall. Later, Antony Gibbs put in his own organ, together with a new entrance with double doors to protect his family from the sound. Removal of the organ some years ago revealed the original stencilling from these 1887–90 alterations.

Furniture

The architectural roll-top desk is perhaps the masterpiece of the Warwick cabinetmaker James Plucknett, but as yet neither the attribution nor the date is documented. Both this desk and the partners' desk also in this room were once in William Gibbs's study in his London house. An old photograph of that room shows the desk without the central roll-top section, which may have been added subsequently by the same cabinetmaker at the request of Antony Gibbs. The four panels on the centre doors depict ancient crafts such as pottery and carpentry, underlining the persistent emphasis on good craftsmanship throughout the house. In the centre is a tablet incised in Latin with a quotation from Horace: 'Let there be a seat for my old age.'

Most of the other Victorian furniture here is by or attributed to Collier and Plucknett. Some pieces may have been commissioned for Charlton in the early 1880s, rather than for Tyntesfield. Together with other fine Plucknett pieces in the Cloister, Dining Room and Billiard Room, Tyntesfield has the largest collection of work by this outstanding Warwick and Leamington Spa firm. From 1872 to 1880 it advertised as 'Collier and Plucknett … upholsterers, cabinet makers and decorators by appointment to Her Majesty, and Manufacturers of rich carved furniture in the peculiar styles characteristic of the Gothic, Tudor and Elizabethan ages.'

The roll-top desk was probably made for William Gibbs

Mrs Gibbs's Room

This room, so different in its decorative detail, was designed specifically for William Gibbs's wife, Matilda Blanche – Blanchey as he called her in his diaries. *The frieze of elaborate boxwood carvings* of exotic fruits and flowers is carved with a rare clarity and consistency of style, which will surely lead to the identity of the artist. The unusual use of fretwork on the door and on the shutters also distinguishes this room from the main reception rooms.

A door, originally to the conservatory lobby, now leads to a tiled garden porch added after the conservatory was demolished in 1917. The naturalistic carvings in the panelling of Blanche's room would have formed a link with the conservatory, in which the pale green glass (following Hooker's palm-house at Kew) would have admitted a distinctive light into the room.

Mrs Gibbs's Room

Should the Trust redecorate?

The discovery, within a few weeks of the National Trust's purchase of Tyntesfield, of the original carpet for this room, carefully rolled and stored away, opens up the exciting possibility of supporting the remarkable panelling with a more sympathetic decorative scheme. Here, an almost archaeological approach might be justified, taking advantage of paint scrapes, possible evidence in old photographs and even the remnants of old stencilling or wallpapers that may be lurking beneath light switches. Compromise would still be necessary, most obviously with the fireplace. In about 1908 George and Via Gibbs removed Norton's original wooden two-tier fireplace, replacing it with a narrower stone one commissioned from Venice, just as they had done in the Drawing Room.

The panelling in Mrs Gibbs's Room is decorated with naturalistic carving

The Billiard Room

When William Gibbs's rebuilding was completed in 1865, he was 75. It was presumably for his four sons, three of whom were still in their teens, that he included this large Billiard Room. But William may also have been remembering his months in Bristol at the age of sixteen working as a clerk in his uncle's business. When there was little work to do, his diaries record long walks and much playing of billiards.

Norton's pine roof is an impressively complex and original structure of dormer windows and hammerbeams that lets in the maximum possible amount of light. Much of the rest of the room, including the strong design of the window's fine tracery, is due to Antony Gibbs's changes of 1887–90 designed by Henry Woodyer.

By the mid-19th century, smoking rooms had begun to be set aside specifically for that purpose. William, however, who had grown up at a time when smoking was largely banished from polite society, permitted smoking only in the uppermost room of the house – in the tower on the third floor on the south front above the children's bedrooms. In the late 1880s, Antony commissioned Woodyer to extend the Billiard Room into the inner courtyard with an inglenook fireplace, and the room now became the official smoking room. The bookcases may have been added at this time.

Furniture

Antony also commissioned the oak *billiard-table*. It bears the prominent label of James Plucknett & Co. and its decorative carving incorporates Antony's initials. The sides depict traditional British sports such as archery, bowls and wrestling. In comparison with other work at Tyntesfield by this firm, the panels are surprisingly clumsy and the figures are stiff. The table was centrally heated and connected directly to the electrically operated scoreboard: pressing a button on the side of the table recorded the score. The oak bureau bookcase with silvered bird handles is by Cox & Sons, about 1875.

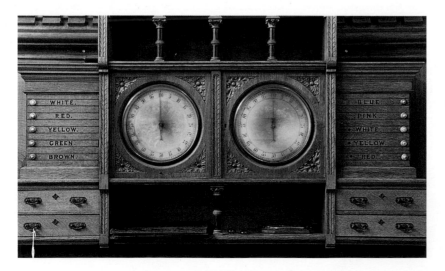

(Above) The moose in the Billiard Room was shot by Via Gibbs in Canada in 1911

(Left) The electric scoreboard for the billiard-table

(Right) The urinal was added by Antony Gibbs

The door at the far end of the room opens to a group of rooms, including the Lathe Room (which William built specifically for Antony), the Gun Room and a WC, which Antony improved with the addition of an early and very decorative urinal. These rooms adjoin the Servants' Hall, above which were the male servants' bedrooms. Unused for decades, until recently these rooms were a summer roost for a colony of lesser horseshoe bats. During 2007 work took place in the garden passage to create new areas for the bats to move to and the National Trust can now start to restore these rooms.

The Drying Room

The Servants' Quarters

The 1891 census records Antony and Janet Gibbs and nine children aged from seventeen to one, together with nineteen servants, all living at Tyntesfield. It is this period of the house's past life that the National Trust may wish most to evoke in both the servants' quarters and in some bedrooms. It might best be characterised by the wardrobes in the children's bedrooms, each carved proudly with the child's initials.

The order and titles of the servants in that census were: butler, two footmen, housekeeper, lady's maid, cook, six house maids, nurse, two nursery maids, still-room maid, two scullery maids, and hall boy. There were also coachmen and grooms living in the stables, and gardeners and gamekeepers in other houses on the estate. Even so, it was a relatively modest establishment by the standards of the day.

(Right) Riding boots packed away on their shoe trees

The layout of the servants' quarters was altered and updated by Antony Gibbs in the late 1880s, but few alterations, except to the bathrooms, have occurred since. The butler's pantries on either side of the massive walk-in safe still have their particular sinks, one lead-lined and one of teak for the safer washing of glass. Nearby, the magnificent original rank of bells, which can still be cranked and rung from some of the rooms, survives, although long ago superseded by an adjoining, but now equally antiquated, electrical system. The Kitchen still has its iron sash-windows and fireproof ceiling. The sequence of three meat larders remains, separating cooked or dressed meat, fresh meat and game. The Still Room, where cakes and preserves would have been made and perhaps the children's drinks prepared, still has its ovens, sinks and cupboards. The Servants' Hall is missing its dining-table, but a very early, if battered, example of linoleum has been found on the floor. Off the courtyard, stores for wood and coal, workshops, brew-house and kennels are little altered, although filled with many of the crucial ingredients of restoration, such as gasoliers and redundant electrical fittings.

Upstairs in the servants' quarters, one is reminded that when the late Lord Wraxall died in 2001, there were no longer any staff living in the house. Many of the servants' upstairs bedrooms, sitting rooms or workrooms had become stores. A serried rank of water cans for carrying hot water to the main bedrooms may be in one room, a dozen wicker baskets for dirty linen in another, and a large group of standing towel rails

The house staff in the late 19th century. Seated by the dog is Hemmings, who remained in service at Tyntesfield until the 1940s

in a third. Although this arrangement was the work of Christie's staff lotting up the contents for sale in 2002, they forcefully express something of the scale of the servants' responsibilities.

Earlier census returns tell us that Anne Sawyer was the housekeeper to William and Blanche Gibbs before she and the butler, James Sawyer, moved into the stables and their son was born. In the absence of any of the Gibbs family from Tyntesfield at the time of two of the later censuses, it is Anne who is described as 'head of household' in 1861, and James who is called 'Domestic Servant in charge of mansion' in 1881. Family diaries and archives are likely to reveal the Sawyers' contribution to the history of Tyntesfield, and we must hope that they and other servants will emerge as personalities.

Decanters and elderly tins in a pantry cupboard

The Chapel

The Chapel presides over almost every view of Tyntesfield, just as the oratory, which preceded it, was at the very centre of the house. Religion was a natural part of daily life at Tyntesfield.

As a young man, William Gibbs was already a devout churchgoer. In 1839 his marriage to Matilda Blanche Crawley-Boevey, whose father and uncle, the Rev. Charles Crawley, were both enthusiastic Tractarians, may have helped to develop William's own deep commitment to the Oxford or High Church Movement, which was to affect the Church of England so profoundly.

William Gibbs's earliest church building project may have been the rebuilding of his wife's parish church at Flaxley in Gloucestershire in 1856 by George Gilbert Scott. The most substantial of the new churches which William paid for in full were those dedicated to St Michael and All Angels at Paddington (1861, Rhode Hawkins), in Bishopston, Bristol (1862, S. T. Welch and J. A. Clark), and in Exeter (1868, Rhode Hawkins). In all, William Gibbs and his family paid for the building or restoration of at least nineteen churches, chapels and cathedrals, as well as supporting innumerable church and other charitable projects.

The most dramatic evidence of William Gibbs's High Church allegiance is Keble College, Oxford. William paid the entire costs of the chapel, built to the designs of William Butterfield between 1873 and 1876. His wife and sons were to pay for the hall, library, common rooms and kitchens, as well as contributing to the endowment of the college. Keble College was conceived as a memorial to John Keble, whose sermon in Oxford in 1833 marked the beginning of the Oxford Movement. William Gibbs wrote of Keble that a 'more sincere, humble minded and devout Christian cannot possibly be imagined'.

(Right) William Gibbs paid for the building of Keble College chapel in Oxford

The Oxford Movement and the principal writers of the *Tracts for the Times*, John Henry Newman, John Keble and Edward Bouverie Pusey, sought to reform the established Church of England in the 1830s. They argued for higher standards of worship, for the beautification of churches, for the revival of the ancient ritual of the early Christian church, and for the wearing of vestments and the singing of hymns. Initially, they strove for a middle way between Roman Catholicism and Low Church evangelicalism, but there were to be bitter controversies, even riots. William and Matilda Blanche Gibbs were never so passionately involved, but they were probably amongst those who were much hurt by Newman's defection to the Roman Catholic Church in 1845.

The Chapel at Tyntesfield was probably the last building in William Gibbs's extraordinary sequence of ecclesiastical patronage. It was built between 1873 and 1875, the year of his death. The architect was Arthur Blomfield, who was the son of a Bishop of London and a prolific designer of High Church churches.

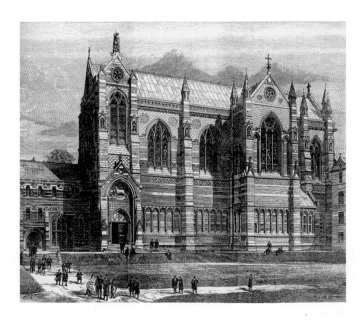

The Chapel

Antony Gibbs may well have witnessed the opening in 1860 of Sir George Gilbert Scott's new chapel for Exeter College, Oxford, which William admired. Both Blomfield's chapel at Tyntesfield and Scott's Exeter College chapel share the same source, the medieval Sainte Chapelle in Paris. At Tyntesfield Blomfield cleverly used the example of the Sainte Chapelle to solve the problem of the extremely awkward site, pressed between the entrance to the servants' courtyard and the steep hillside. The nave and chancel are at first-floor level. The family gained access from the house by means of the covered bridge with internal steps to resolve the difference in height between the first floor and the Chapel floor. The servants could enter from below by a spiral staircase at the entrance to the yard, and the priest could walk down from the Chaplain's House and enter by the north door.

The census returns reveal that there was already a priest living at Tyntesfield in 1871, John B. Medley, who is still listed in the 1891 census. But it is the Rev. John Hardie who served as chaplain and appears in several family photographs in the later 1870s and '80s.

Mosaics

The floor, like the stained glass, was by Powell & Sons and deserves particular attention. It gathers pace and preciousness of materials as it approaches the altar. On the chancel floor a pale blue faience is added to the coloured marbles, and there are small squares of a marvellous honey-coloured Mexican onyx. Around the altar there are squares of bluejohn, the rare Derbyshire fluorspar more often used for precious vases. The mosaics beyond the altar are by Salviati & Co., and the panel of the head of Christ after Leonardo's *Last Supper* was designed by Sir William Boxall, the artist of several of the family portraits.

Furnishings

The Chapel is a remarkably complete example of High Victorian ecclesiastical craftsmanship. But it is also a glittering spiritual envelope in

(Right) A mosaic panel by Salviati behind the altar

need of lighted candles, flowers, vestments, kneelers, silk markers hanging from the Gospels on the lectern, and perhaps an altar frontal, chalice veil and other details of High Church Anglicanism. They are still at Tyntesfield.

At the north door the priest passed the beautiful filigree wrought-iron gate designed by Blomfield and made by the metalworkers Barkentin & Krall, who also made the gem-encrusted cross to the memory of William Gibbs. Powell & Sons made the stained-glass windows. Those in the nave are by Henry Ellis Wooldridge, one of the best stained-glass designers of the day. The ornate wrought-iron screen and gates are by James Lever, of Maidenhead, as is the eagle lectern. Lever also made four brass gas coronas or chandeliers, of which only two remain, with their arms now turned downwards after conversion to electricity. Hart, Son & Peard made the altar candlesticks and alms dish. James Forsyth, who also worked at Cragside in Northumberland, did the stone carving, and G. W. Booth designed the prie-dieu chairs.

The splendid chalice, discreetly set with precious stones, and the altar flagon were both designed by William Butterfield and are dated 1876 (purchased from the estate of the 2nd Lord Wraxall by the National Art Collections Fund and presented to the National Trust).

A memorial

William Gibbs died very soon after the completion of the Chapel. His friend, Sir Arthur Elton of nearby Clevedon Court (also the property of the National Trust), had attended evensong in the Chapel just a few weeks earlier and wrote in his diary on 3 April 1875: 'The good old man – holy and devout – Wm. Gibbs died today.' A few days later, some of the mourners were to be disappointed by the modesty of the funeral. Instead of a grand cortège, the coffin was carried by a relay of 30 estate workers and servants the two miles to Wraxall church.

The Tyntesfield chalice and altar flagon were designed by William Butterfield in 1876

Tyntesfield itself is now a memorial to William Gibbs, as well as a monument to that great Victorian age, when wealth and confidence went hand-in-hand with a deeply felt and public-spirited benevolence.

The most impressive and moving monument to William Gibbs is in the church he had built in Exeter. There, his marble effigy depicts him with a flowing white beard clasping a bible and clad only in a winding sheet. It is inscribed:

William Gibbs, a merchant of London, but by parentage and affection a man of Devon, in his life did many good works for the love of Christ, as elsewhere, so especially in the city of Exeter. One such work – the erection of the Church of SS. Michael and All Angels for the use of the poor of the neighbourhood – is here recorded by his widow and surviving children, to the end that the remembrance of his loving-kindness and piety may not pass away.

The Garden

Early pictures of Tyntesfield, perhaps from the 1840s, show flower-beds close to the house and sloping lawns running into parkland, very much in the manner of Humphry Repton. Most of the present layout was created by William and Blanche Gibbs. In the ensuing 135 years there were even fewer alterations due to changes of taste than inside the house. Moreover, it was to the care of the garden and especially of the trees that the late Lord Wraxall devoted his particular enthusiasm and expertise.

The top and lower terraces, the Broad Walk on the west side, the lake and Paradise were probably created in the 1850s. The rows of differing species of holly, a parade of perfect darning-mushrooms, are a later replacement. There is evidence of payments to the Exeter nurseryman James Veitch in the 1840s, and around 1850 William and Blanche probably consulted the architect and garden designer Alexander Roos.

Above the Broad Walk are carefully maintained vistas up Bendle Combe, and, further along, in quiet seclusion, is the Old Rose Garden with a pattern of box hedges and two thatched, prettily tiled and alarmingly dilapidated summer-houses. The restorable remnants of a Victorian wild garden are on the nearby bank. At the end of the Broad Walk is the arboretum of specimen trees on undulating

Garden terraces were laid out below the south front of the house

The view from the house south over the garden and park to the valley and hills beyond

lawns, called Paradise on the Ordnance Survey map of 1883.

The rose garden is overlooked by two Redwood trees, planted 150 years ago. Elsewhere, amongst a great variety of tree planting that ensures remarkable contrasts of colour even in high summer, William and Blanche included several Cedars of Lebanon. These were grown from seed brought from the Lebanon itself (as recorded on a zinc plaque) and, however fashionable, they were no doubt also a conscious link with the Holy Land.

To the west of the house, adjoining the Billiard Room was John Norton's impressive conservatory, which replaced an earlier and smaller hot-house in the Gothic style. The central feature of Norton's building was an octagon rising into an onion-shaped dome with a gilt copper cupola, based upon the dome of St Mark's in Venice. It was demolished in or before 1917, but its footprint can still be seen on the ground, together with a rather forlorn, but surviving, palm tree. The wooden aviary nearby is on the point of collapse. Against the south front of the Drawing Room is the striking veranda probably added for Blanche Gibbs in 1885 to the designs of Henry Woodyer.

The Gothic terrace balustrades, flights of steps and architectural seats closing vistas along the walks were probably added after 1883. The lower terrace in the front of the house has eight formal flower-beds, each with a white marble urn at its centre surrounded by circular hollies. Regularly and diligently clipped for over a hundred years, the hollies have surreptitiously expanded both out and up and they now obscure the bases of the urns and too much of the beds.

From the lower terrace a double flight of steps brings you to the long middle walk lined with jaunty, even drunken, Irish yews, some of which were once interspersed with yuccas. It was extended westwards past the lake after 1883. Further down still is the lower walk of Portugal laurels, now formed into a tunnel. At the lake's western end there is a collection of azaleas planted in 1910. Even if some of the azaleas prove to be of North American origin, they would, at the time, have been perceived as Japanese and as exotic as the collections of oriental porcelain in the house.

The view from the upper terrace makes an effortless transition from the garden, over a ha-ha, across the park to the valley and distant hills and, on a clear day, to beyond Steepholm in the Bristol Channel. The house seems to fit into its setting with peculiar ease. The formality of the surrounding terraces, the picturesque outline and balanced asymmetry of each frontage, the naturalism of the carving both inside and out, and the encircling and overhanging woods – all these factors contribute to the effect.

More information is available in the garden leaflet, available from the House, Visitor Reception and Shop.

The Estate

The National Trust was able to acquire only a quarter of the Tyntesfield estate (the shaded area on the map opposite), but that quarter is probably only a little smaller than the portion of land purchased by William Gibbs in 1843. William steadily increased the estate to over 3,000 acres (1,214 hectares), nearly 2,000 (809 hectares) of which remained in 2002.

Whether you arrive at Tyntesfield from the north or the south, you pass modest gatehouses, Clevedon Lodge or Wraxall Lodge, built in an unpretentious country-cottage manner. The gates bearing the St Kilda sheep of the 1st Lord Wraxall's coat of arms are of 1968. In William Gibbs's day, timber gates had internal windlasses so that they appeared to operate of their own accord. His commitment to modern technology was allied to a genuine concern for the welfare of the family's servants and estate workers.

Between the south gatehouse and the mansion are what the *Builder* called in 1866 'intermediate lodges for domestic servants'. To the north of the Chapel are the Chaplain's Lodge and the larger, Chaplain's House added after 1883, possibly designed by Henry Woodyer. But unseen from the entrance drives are the stables and stable yard, the kitchen gardens and gardeners' cottages and the Home Farm with its large and 'model' dairy parlour, builders' yard and carpenters' shop. All take careful advantage of folds in the hillside.

After the rebuilding of Tyntesfield in the early 1860s, the mansion, offices and lodges were lit by gas, supplied from a gasometer, disguised by a small plantation near the kitchen garden. The present project office building may have housed the controls. Hidden in the woods a hundred yards above the Chapel are

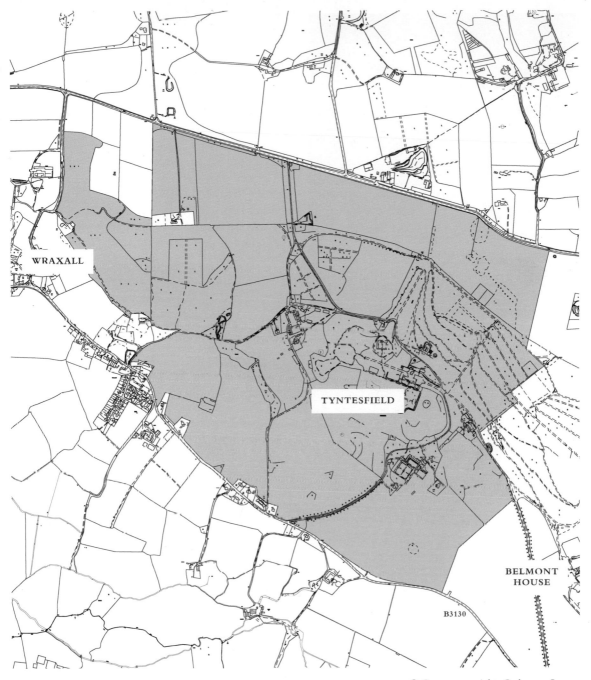

WRAXALL

TYNTESFIELD

BELMONT
HOUSE

B3130

(Left) The stables

the surviving sawmill and yard and the accumulator building, where electricity was generated and stored after it had succeeded gas lighting in 1890. At the top of the hill there was a water-catch – an acre of asphalted ground collected rainwater, which was piped to the house, supplying water closets, baths and early fire hydrants on each floor. The mansion's hot-air heating was supplied through vents from the three coal-fired boilers in the basement. It extended only to the principal rooms on the ground floor, including the Hall, corridors and conservatory of the house.

The stables and stable yard, together with the accommodation for grooms and coachmen and

(Left) The horse trough in the stable courtyard was designed by Henry Woodyer

(Below) The greenhouses remain in production

for the butler and his wife, were all remodelled by Woodyer for Antony Gibbs in 1888. The elaborate iron lamps on the entrance piers and the charming fountain and horse trough are typical of his idiosyncratic work.

Increasingly through the 19th century, the kitchen garden was on show to the family and their guests. Perhaps with this in mind, Antony Gibbs made major alterations and additions. The kitchen garden was now entered through an ornamental wrought-iron gate, dated 1896, and an Italianate loggia. A stone and brick orangery and working buildings screening the walled gardens were added. The architect was probably Walter Cave, a former pupil of Sir Arthur Blomfield. Antony Gibbs replaced his father's timber houses with metal-framed houses purchased from Walter MacFarlane & Co., the

(Right) The wrought-iron gate to the kitchen garden, erected in 1896, bears the family motto 'tenax propositi' ('tenacious of purpose')

glass being secured by G. Beard and Sons' patented glazing system, which did not require the use of putty. Completion of these changes commemorated Queen Victoria's Diamond Jubilee of 1897.

The kitchen gardens at Tyntesfield are among the very few Victorian walled gardens to have remained in continuous cultivation since they were built. Only after the late Lord Wraxall's death was part of the large walled garden grassed over and some of the espaliered fruit trees removed. However, in August 2002, one of the most cheering demonstrations of the enduring vitality of this estate and of the smooth transition from private to public ownership was the continued appearance in the scullery every Thursday afternoon of a small cartload of cut flowers and fresh vegetables. Today, produce is available in the kitchen garden.

(Left) The orangery

The Gibbs Family

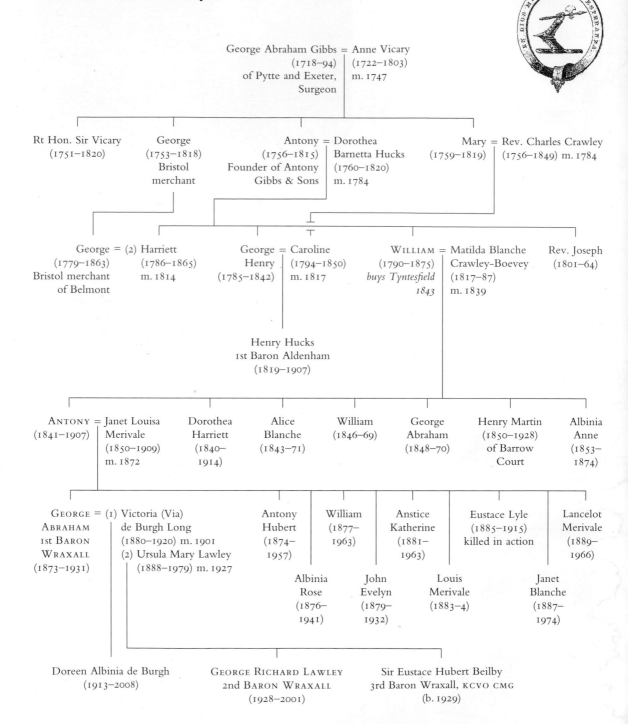

George Abraham Gibbs = Anne Vicary
(1718–94)　(1722–1803)
of Pytte and Exeter,　m. 1747
Surgeon

Rt Hon. Sir Vicary
(1751–1820)

George
(1753–1818)
Bristol
merchant

Antony = Dorothea
(1756–1815)　Barnetta Hucks
Founder of Antony　(1760–1820)
Gibbs & Sons　m. 1784

Mary = Rev. Charles Crawley
(1759–1819)　(1756–1849) m. 1784

George = (2) Harriett
(1779–1863)　(1786–1865)
Bristol merchant　m. 1814
of Belmont

George = Caroline
Henry　(1794–1850)
(1785–1842)　m. 1817

WILLIAM = Matilda Blanche
(1790–1875)　Crawley-Boevey
buys Tyntesfield　(1817–87)
1843　m. 1839

Rev. Joseph
(1801–64)

Henry Hucks
1st Baron Aldenham
(1819–1907)

ANTONY = Janet Louisa
(1841–1907)　Merivale
(1850–1909)
m. 1872

Dorothea
Harriett
(1840–
1914)

Alice
Blanche
(1843–71)

William
(1846–69)

George
Abraham
(1848–70)

Henry Martin
(1850–1928)
of Barrow
Court

Albinia
Anne
(1853–
1874)

GEORGE = (1) Victoria (Via)
ABRAHAM　de Burgh Long
1st BARON　(1880–1920) m. 1901
WRAXALL　(2) Ursula Mary Lawley
(1873–1931)　　(1888–1979) m. 1927

Antony
Hubert
(1874–
1957)

William
(1877–
1963)

Anstice
Katherine
(1881–
1963)

Eustace Lyle
(1885–1915)
killed in action

Lancelot
Merivale
(1889–
1966)

Albinia
Rose
(1876–
1941)

John
Evelyn
(1879–
1932)

Louis
Merivale
(1883–4)

Janet
Blanche
(1887–
1974)

Doreen Albinia de Burgh
(1913–2008)

GEORGE RICHARD LAWLEY
2nd BARON WRAXALL
(1928–2001)

Sir Eustace Hubert Beilby
3rd Baron Wraxall, KCVO CMG
(b. 1929)

Owners of Tyntesfield in CAPITALS